MW01612066

"I love this book. The introduction alone I have read at least five times privately, and once to my family, and once to the elders at our church. The thoughts you find there establish the template for the book, which is full of thoughtful and warm-hearted insights that will help you keep Jesus Christ at the center of your life. Miss whatever you have to, but don't go missing Jesus, and don't miss out on this book."

— **Milton Vincent, pastor of Cornerstone Fellowship Bible Church, Riverside, CA and author of *A Gospel Primer for Christians: Learning to See the Glories of God's Love***

"We have to be consistently reminded that the gospel is not just the way in, it's the way through; indeed, it's the destination! Through the power of sound theology and the real life stories of Jesus' followers, the Morrises underline what Jesus taught on the road to Emmaus – that the Scriptures preeminently concern him. The Morrises remind us that the gospel of Jesus Christ doesn't just accomplish our justification; it powers our sanctification as well, as we, not missing him, fix our eyes on Jesus."

— **Ted Hamilton, Senior pastor, New Life Presbyterian Church, Escondido, CA**

"The Morrises see that many professed Christians actually keep Christ at a distance, to their own loss. But the stories told here, vivid, poignant, and searching as they are, should bring him and us close."

— **J. I. Packer, professor of theology at Regent College and author of *Knowing God***

"Charles and Janet have written an encouraging book. And the Lord knows we need encouragement! Their gentle pursuit of a grace-filled life will reorient your soul. This book will not only warm your heart but brace you for the chill of a post-Christian world."

— **Paul Miller, founder of seeJesus Ministries and author of *A Praying Life***

"Behind the unobtrusive cover and inconspicuous title is a sweet book that offers profound answers to one of life's most common experiences. If you feel like you're missing out, or you're convinced that you're missing Jesus, get it and read it. You won't be sorry."

—TIM CHALLIES, blogger, author, and book reviewer

"For too many years I thought that the storyline of the Bible was primarily about me—at first about how I could get what I wanted, and then later about how I was doing on the road of my personal transformation. And then Jesus showed up and began to teach me that he is the Story, that he is the subject of all the verbs. *Missing Jesus* is a book where you will find him, and in the most surprising yet ordinary places: at a graveside, on a dirt road, in the cracking of a crust of bread. I love this book and wholeheartedly recommend it."

—ELYSE FITZPATRICK, biblical counselor, women's ministry leader, and author of *Found in Him: The Joy of the Incarnation and Our Union with Christ*

MISSING JESUS

DISCUSSION GUIDE

Find Your
Life in His
Great Story

BY CHARLES & JANET MORRIS

WITH CYNDI ANDERSON

This discussion guide is for individual or group study, intended for use with "Missing Jesus—Find Your Life in His Great Story" By Charles and Janet Morris (2014) Moody Publishers.

ISBN 978-0-578-14425-2

Quotes from "Missing Jesus" are in regular *italics*; pages and Kindle locations cited.

All Scripture references are in ***bold italics.*** Use any preferred Bible translation to answer the question.

Q = Questions suitable for group discussion
📖 = Read aloud for group discussion

Time Alone With Jesus segment is for personal reflection and prayer

The chapters in Missing Jesus are divided into the following three themes:

PART ONE
SEEING HIM BIG

We *Miss Jesus* because we see him small;
we *Find Him* in the fullness of his glory.

PART TWO
BEING THE GUEST

We *Miss Jesus* because we see the gospel small;
we *Find Him* in the fullness of his grace.

PART THREE:
MAKING HIS GLORY KNOWN

We *Miss Jesus* because we are living small;
we *Find Him* in the glory of our calling.

Suggested opportunities for small group discussion of *Missing Jesus:*

- Home fellowship groups
- Adult education classes
- Men's or women's Bible studies
- One-on-one evangelism or discipleship
- Campus ministry
- Community outreach

"For where two or three have gathered together in My name, I am there in their midst."

– Matthew 18:20

The two disciples on the road to Emmaus were discussing Jesus with each other when Jesus himself came and began walking alongside them. As they discussed him, Jesus showed up and asked, "What are you discussing as you walk along?" He listened to their confounded narration of recent events and then opened the scriptures concerning himself. The Living Word himself revealed the Word of God to them! And later, as the Bread of Heaven himself broke bread with them, he opened their eyes and they recognized him.

So, why a discussion guide for *Missing Jesus*? Because where two or three gather in Jesus' name—discussing him—he shows up and our eyes are opened. *Missing Jesus* is a book that is <u>all</u> about Jesus. The discussion guide was developed as an aid for small groups to discuss the wonders of Jesus and, as you discuss him, to see him as he is.

"Jesus is not one of many lights. Jesus is the Sun. When we see his cosmic significance it reorders our world. The weight of his glory starts to outweigh everything else. It delivers us out of our small way of life into a wide and joyous orbit of worship." – Page 23, *Missing Jesus*

The scriptures in the discussion guide were selected to direct the conversation toward Jesus through his Word. The "Time Alone With Jesus" tool for each chapter is meant for personal reflection, but can also be used to direct small group prayer time. Our prayer is that through intentional, focused, and honest discussion concerning Jesus, you won't miss him.

It's <u>all</u> about Jesus!
CHARLES AND JANET MORRIS
CYNDI ANDERSON

Part 1

SEEING HIM BIG

CHAPTER ONE
Who is Worthy of My Life?

1. Q How do you relate to any of the descriptions in the first chapter of what it's like to miss Jesus?

2. *"I can live small—and when I do I reduce Jesus."* (P 17; Kindle loc 156)
   Q What does it mean to "live small," and how does doing so "reduce Jesus"?

3. 📖 Read the story of the West Asian woman that Charles and Janet met in London:
   We needed Jesus to break into our hearts the day we were out on that rainy sidewalk in London and he did, right then and there, in a way we didn't expect. A young West Asian woman slowed down, took one of our tracts, and paused as she read the title, "Have You Ever Wanted a New Life?" Janet said, "It's about Jesus. Do you know about Jesus?"
   "Not much," she said, "but I've been looking for someone who's worthy of my life." "Well, that would definitely be Jesus," Janet told her. She nodded her thanks and began reading as she went on her way, leaving us to marvel that someone who didn't even know him would use that biblical word worthy. We rolled it around in our hearts. Who is worthy of our lives? Who

but Jesus? According to the Bible, the entire universe is singing "worthy" to him and that young woman's comment made it real to us again. He is the only one who is worthy, not only of our lives, but of everything in all of creation. It was like waking from a trance.

We need to wake from that trance. We need his glory to keep on breaking into our hearts and waking us up, because when we see his glory it changes everything. (Pp 17-18; Kindle loc 162-168)

    Q Think about your own life. What are the things you feel you need, that you strive to achieve, that make or break your day? Are you giving your life away to unworthy things?

    Q Why is Jesus the only one worthy of our life?

4. A spiritual Copernican Revolution occurs when our worldview shifts from being "all about me" to being "all about Jesus." (Pp 20-21; Kindle loc 199-217)

    Q In what way(s) does this shift change everything else?

    Q In what area(s) do you see a need for an <u>ongoing</u> Copernican Revolution in your own life?

5. 📖 Read the excerpt below about different spiritualities:

The world we live in is not much different. John wrote his gospel in the midst of a pagan world where gaining "light" was a universal spiritual concern. It's the same today. People are groping in the darkness and our

Western world has turned East for spiritual answers. Buddha supposedly once said, "If you see the Buddha in the road, shoot him." A Buddhist-leaning friend of ours explained that this is a warning not to let anyone intrude himself into your search for spiritual light. Everything has to be cleared away, every thought, every person, every preconceived notion, so you can find your own way. We're being told this in one form or another all the time. This same spiritual message is being woven all through our culture and it never challenges our centrality; it only reinforces it.

Jesus does just the opposite. He puts himself squarely in our road and points to himself and says, "Look to me. I am the light of the world." The world is telling us we have a divine spark within us; that we just need to be true to ourselves. It's flattering but we need to be clear that Jesus is flatly contradicting this assertion and all the spiritual systems that teach it. He says that, to the contrary, we're actually filled with deep darkness. We need the light to shine into our hearts and bring us to life and he is that light. The pluralistic world doesn't want to hear this message but there wasn't a hateful bone in Jesus' body when he said it, only love willing to affront our pride so we could be saved.

Jesus is not one of many lights. Jesus is the Sun. When we see his cosmic significance it reorders our world. The weight of his glory starts to outweigh everything else. It delivers us out of our small way of life into a wide and joyous orbit of worship. (P 23; Kindle loc 241-255)

Q In what way(s) do you see *"this same spiritual message being woven all through our culture"*?

Q Compare and contrast the Eastern notion of seeking the "light" or "divine spark" within us vs. seeking the Light of the World—Jesus. How would you respond to those who say that all religions are basically the same?

6. Q In the story of Darrell Johnson on pages 21-24 (Kindle loc 218-262), how did Darrell finally come to answer the question, "Who does Jesus say he is?"

Q Who do you say that he is?

7. 📖 Read *John 12:23-35*. Jesus refers to his death as the "hour" when he will "be glorified." (v 23)
    Q Find ways in this passage that the cross glorifies Jesus.

Q How does the cross "draw" you to Jesus? (v 32)

TIME ALONE WITH JESUS: Just before he went to the cross, Jesus told his Father he wanted those who believed in him to "see his glory." As you begin this study, write a prayer asking the Lord to show you his glory. You can be confident that he will do this because it's what he wants, too!

CHAPTER TWO

Living in the Great Story

1. Listen to your Father tell you a story—the Great Story.
   - Q Whose story is it?
   - Q Who is the main character?
   - Q What is the main theme?
   - Q What is the beginning?
   - Q What is the end?

2. Q How does embracing the Great Story change how you view your own story (your life, what's important, your purpose, your identity, your struggles or suffering)?

   Q How has God re-enacted the gospel story in your life?

3. Read the story of Sally Lloyd Jones, author of *The Jesus Storybook Bible.* (Pp 31-32; Kindle loc 351-375)
   - Q Compare and contrast viewing Jesus as the heroic thread throughout all the stories in the Bible vs. viewing the Bible as stories of people we should imitate.

4. 📖 Read the section on "another story" below:
   But there's another story. Our enemy is spinning another tale, one where God is out of the picture and we're endowed with the inalienable right to live as we choose. Ultimately there are only two stories: God's story or the enemy's story, the story that brings life or the story that brings death, the truth or the lie.

   Some version of the lie is coming at us all the time, in a thousand different guises, but they all have this in common—they put us at the center and say, "Once upon a time there was you and it's all about you." Open any magazine, listen to any talk show, go in to any bookstore and you'll hear that story. It can come in the form of a promise that our individual dream is meant to come true or it can be a full-blown myth, a sweeping tale of where we come from and where we're headed. (P 33; Kindle loc 375-408)

Q Share the versions (or "-isms") of the great lie and its effect that you see every day around you.

Q How have you seen this lie affect you and those you love?

Q How does God's gift of his Son answer that lie?

5. Q What strikes you about the way God gradually revealed his story to Ridley Herschell, a Jewish believer? (Pp 35-36; Kindle loc 408-451)

Q How has God gradually revealed his story to you?

6. Read **Philippians 4:4-7, 12-13.** Learning gratitude played a major role in Ann Voskamp's story. (Pp 37-39; Kindle loc 451-485)

Q How can we miss the grace of God's story—miss Jesus— until we learn to cultivate the practice of gratitude?

TIME ALONE WITH JESUS: As you listen to the Father's Great Story, begin by naming and giving him thanks for his lavish blessings in Jesus in the space below. Ask him to show you the wonder of being part of this Great Story that's all about Jesus!

CHAPTER THREE
The Work of One Who Lives

1. Q In what various ways did the reality of Jesus' presence meet Charles and Janet when the reality of Jeff's death hit them hard? (Pp 42-44; Kindle loc 504-519)

2. 📖 *"For almost two thousand years the church has declared, 'He is risen,' and in response has thundered back, 'He is risen indeed!'"* (P 43; Kindle loc 531)

   Q Even though you can't see him with your physical eyes, when and where have you seen Jesus alive through the eyes of faith?

3. 📖 Read *Isaiah 9:2.* Jesus—the Light of the World—is alive and powerfully at work. The place we can see this most strikingly is in the transformed lives of his people.

   Q What impressed you most about the transformation from darkness into the light in:

   a. The Malawian people, (Pp 47-48; Kindle loc 585-617) and/or

   b. Charles and Janet's son, Peter, (Pp 49-51; Kindle loc 622-653) and/or

   c. Rosaria Butterfield? (Pp 52-54; Kindle loc 673-716)

4. 📖 Read the quote by Athanasius on page 51 (Kindle loc 657-662).
Look at the facts of the case. The Savior is working mightily among men, every day. He is invisibly persuading numbers of people all over the world to accept his faith and be obedient to his teaching. Can anyone in the face of this still doubt that he has risen and lives ... ? Does a dead man prick the consciences of men so they throw all the traditions of their fathers to the winds and bow down before the teaching of Christ? If he is no longer active in the world ... how is it that he makes the adulterer [cease] from his adultery, the murderer from murdering ... ? This is the work of one who lives, not of the dead; and more than that, it is the work of God.

   Q How does knowing that Jesus is alive and real—not just a dead martyr, an inspirational historical figure whose teachings we follow, or a person from the past after whom we pattern our lives, but one who lives today—empower us to pray expectantly?

   Q For what or whom do you need to pray expectantly right now?

TIME ALONE WITH JESUS: Ask the Lord to give you a greater awareness of the transforming power of Jesus' resurrection. Also ask him for the eyes of faith to pray expectantly and to see the answers. Pray and expect!

Part 2

BEING THE GUEST

CHAPTER FOUR
Relaxing in Him

1. Q What does Dr. Packer mean when he says, "*I have learned that
   Jesus is not Jeeves*"? (P 59; Kindle loc 735-744)

2. Read Janet's account of how she learned that "Jesus is not Jeeves."
   (Pp 60-62; Kindle loc 744-785)
   Q How do you relate to her story in your own experience?

   Q How does learning that God is not a cosmic valet lead to
   the fear of the Lord?

   Q Where do you find refuge?

3. Q What made Linda's story of the discarded law books such a great
   illustration of how we feel under the weight of the law? (P 66;
   Kindle loc 831-849)

   Q How do you relate to this illustration?

4. 📖 Read the parable of the Prodigal in *Luke 15:11-32*.
   Q In what way(s) does the older son reflect the weight of the
   law's gavel as he bristles with disapproval and despises the
   father's grace that is freely offered to his younger brother?

Q Have you ever felt this weight in the way you view the Christian life, or from others?

Q In what way(s) is Jesus our True Older Brother?

Q How does this relationship free us to serve and enjoy him in love and gratitude rather than performing out of fear?

5. Twice, God pronounced over Jesus—once at his baptism and again at his transfiguration—these words, "This is my Beloved Son, in whom I am well-pleased." The verdict is in and, if you are in Christ, the Father is saying the same of you.
   Q What is your first response to this?

6. 📖 *"Justification is a universal issue"* (P 70; Kindle loc 904)—even among non-Christians and atheists.
   Q What are some of the various ways people address this "issue" by justifying themselves?

   📖 Read *Romans 5:1-2, 6-11, 18.*
   Q How did Jesus deal with the issue of justification once and for all?

TIME ALONE WITH JESUS: Ask the Lord to show you way(s) that you may yet be viewing Jesus as a cosmic "valet." Repent of your presumption, and ask him to help you to see him clearly as he is.

If you are still living your life "in the courtroom," ask the Lord to show you that Jesus is your Advocate—the True Older Brother—and begin to relax in the righteousness that is in him alone.

CHAPTER FIVE
The Passing of the Eclipse

1. 📖 *"The Father is singing his song of love over every one of his children but not all of us are hearing it. For some of us, our heavenly Father is a blank, a face we can't seem to see. We live like orphans, harassed and worn out by the requirements of life, because we have no sense of our Father's love."* (Pp 78-79; Kindle loc 1009-1013)

    Q In what way(s) does your relationship with your earthly father give you a sense of your heavenly Father's love, and/or

    Q In what way(s) does your relationship with your earthly father make sensing your heavenly Father's love more difficult?

2. Q Describe your understanding of how your Father God views you.

3. At various times, Jesus told his disciples that to see him was to see his Father.

    Q Have you ever considered Jesus as the "nice one" and God the Father as the "stern, unapproachable one"? (P 80; Kindle loc 1034-1039)

    📖 Read *John 5:19.*

    Q Think of the ways Jesus demonstrated his heart of love in his earthly ministry. How does this verse affect your view of the face and heart of God?

4. 📖 Read this excerpt about the Father's love revealed in his Son:

Jesus entered into our pain with so much compassion it broke his heart. But he wants us to understand that this is also our Father's compassion. He does not want us to miss this so before he raised Lazarus from the dead he prayed, "Father, I thank you that you have heard me. I knew that you always hear me, but I said this for the benefit of the people standing here, that they may believe that you sent me."

We can see our Father's face in Jesus—in his compassion, his kindness, his willingness to feed, and heal, and teach but we can see it most clearly on the cross. That's where the full force of our Father's love comes blazing forth. When Jesus was in the upper room talking to his disciples he told them, "If you really know me, you will know my Father as well. From now on, you do know him and have seen him." (Pp 81-82; Kindle loc 1044-1058)

Q How do we see the Father's face and heart most clearly on the cross?

5. Jesus not only taught his disciples to pray, "Our Father," but he also made calling God our Father possible.

Q How did this factor into the conversion story of Bilquis Sheikh, a former Muslim? (Pp 83-85; Kindle loc 1077-1091)

6. 📖 Read the story of "Daddy-Long-Legs" below:

When I read Jean Webster's classic novel "Daddy-Long-Legs" a few years ago I thought, "This really captures the longing I have for a close connection with my heavenly Father." It's the story of Jerusha Abbott, who was the oldest orphan in the orphanage. Every Wednesday when the trustees came to visit she had to wipe the noses of the other ninety-seven orphans and make sure they were starched and presentable. One Wednesday after being on her feet since five in the morning, "doing everybody's bidding," she was leaning against the window watching the carriages leave, following them in her imagination to the big houses on the hillside. She was just thinking what it would be like to be able to say "home," when her daydreams were interrupted by a summons to the matron's office.

Thankfully, instead of the reprimand she was expecting, Mrs. Lippet gave her a piece of good news. One of the trustees had decided to pay her way to college. His monetary provision was very generous, too generous in Matron's opinion, but he did have two stipulations: she was never to know his name and she was required to write him a long letter every week. Jerusha had almost caught a glimpse of her benefactor as she was coming into Matron's office and he was leaving, but she only saw his elongated shadow against the wall. From then on she referred to him as "Daddy-Long-Legs." (P 88; Kindle loc 1152-1162)

Q How does this story illustrate:

- The longing we have for a close connection to our heavenly Father, and/or

- The way in which we pray like the pagans (to someone we don't know and don't know if he's listening)?

TIME ALONE WITH JESUS: Read the following verses and write down words or phrases that tell how the Father sees you:
Matthew 6:25-32

Matthew 7:7-11

Luke 12:32

Let his words enrich and embolden your prayer to your heavenly Father as you enjoy your time with him.

Puritan writer John Owen said, *"The greatest sorrow and burden you can lay on the Father, the greatest unkindness you can do to him, is not to believe that he loves you."* (P 89; Kindle loc 1171) Will you believe that he loves <u>you</u>?

CHAPTER SIX
The Great Dilemma

1. Read pages 93-95 (Kindle loc 1227-1264).

   Q Summarize the great dilemma of becoming more self-focused while attempting to be more holy—or as Augustine called it *incurvatas in se*.

2. No one was more righteous based on the law than Paul was as Saul, the Pharisee, before his conversion.

   📖 Read **Romans 7:14-25**.

   Q How does Paul describe the dilemma of self-effort in pursuing righteousness?

3. Q What makes the story of the Christian speaker in Pensacola, Florida so powerful? (P 98; Kindle loc 1301-1310)

4. Q What makes it so *"hard to throw our self-righteousness away—especially if we think we've chalked up some points"*? (P 99; Kindle 1323)

5. Q Why do *"self-righteousness and pride have to go if we want to have Jesus"?* (P 100; Kindle loc 1332)

6. Q When Jesus becomes the consuming object in your life, how does it answer the great dilemma?

TIME ALONE WITH JESUS: Ask the Lord to give you the opportunity and desire this week to share your faith in a way that glorifies Jesus— to direct the attention away from yourself and on to him, your "consuming object."

Read *Psalm 29:1-2* aloud. Admit to Jesus that you have no virtue and ascribe it all to him. Draw your life from him.

CHAPTER SEVEN
Keeping in Step

1. Read the story of Charles and Janet's Christmas vacation. (Pp 105 106; Kindle loc 1386-1409) In **John 15:5**, Jesus said, "apart from me you can do nothing."
   Q How does Charles' story illustrate this truth?

2. Q Since the law of Christ is love, why do *"we especially need the Spirit to empower us to love"?* (P 108; Kindle loc 1439)

   Q What makes real, sacrificial love nearly impossible to accomplish in the flesh?

   Q What person do you specifically need the Spirit's power in order to love better?

3. Read **Galatians 5:16-24.**
   These <u>are not</u> two lists that tell us:
   a. Don't do these things (19-21), but

   b. Do these other things instead (22-23).

   These <u>are</u> two lists that tell us:
   a. Deeds that result from relying on our flesh (19-21), and

   b. The result, or "fruit," of relying on the Spirit (22-23).

We can try to imitate the fruit of the Spirit through self-effort, but it won't produce the work of the Spirit, and may even result in becoming "conceited, provoking one another or envying one another." (v 26).

Q How does this encourage and challenge you to rely on the Spirit's work in you?

4. Read the story of Charles and the ruined tomatoes. (Pp 109-111; Kindle loc 1455-1485)

Q What fruit did the Spirit produce in him?

Q How did Charles' Spirit-produced response differ from conventional anger management accomplished in the flesh?

5. *"Spirit-people are gospel-transformed people."* (P 112; Kindle loc 1499)

Q What role does the gospel have in teaching us to "keep in step with the Spirit"? (Galatians 5:25)

6. ⌸ Read the following excerpt on page 112-113 (Kindle loc 1502):
Paul told the Corinthians, "I am in the law of Christ." Christ's laid-down life of love had become the apostle's rule of life. It was shaping the way he lived. He was willing to become "all things to all people in order to save some" because he knew the Son of God had done that for him. He didn't just know it; he was encompassed by it, shaped by it, called by it. He laid down his own identity so he could freely identify with all kinds of people and he did it because Christ had identified with him. That's the kind of thinking we're meant to be doing—we're meant to connect the dots between how we've been loved and how we're called to love. The only thing that counts, Paul says, is "faith expressing itself in love" (Gal. 5:6 NLT).

The Macedonians are another example of how this works. Paul encouraged them to take up an offering for the poor in Jerusalem and he says they "exceeded his expectations" because "they gave themselves first of all to the Lord." They didn't just dig in their pockets; they gave their very lives to Jesus and then "gave as much as they were able and even beyond their ability." Why did they do this? Because they were full of the gospel.

Q What does keeping "in step with the Spirit" look like?

TIME ALONE WITH JESUS: As a believer, "*You can live kata sarka—according to the flesh—or you can live kata pneuma—according to the Spirit.*" (P 106; Kindle loc 1406-1407)

In what area are you struggling to walk in the Spirit?

Have you been trying to manage your sin or imitate spiritual fruit by relying on your flesh?

Ask the Lord to teach you to "keep in step with the Spirit" and to transform you day-by-day through the gospel. Believer! You <u>can</u> live *kata pneuma*!

Part 3

MAKING HIS GLORY KNOWN

CHAPTER EIGHT
The Reconciling Things

1. Q [Optional icebreaker for small groups] What are some of the things you look for in a church home?

2. *"Greetings. My name is Jack Miller and I am a recovering Pharisee ... and you're one, too, but don't worry—Jesus is a great Savior."* (P 118; Kindle loc 1551)

    Q What strikes you most about this pastor's greeting?

    Q What is it that makes us like the self-righteous Pharisees?

    Q Why is our only hope of recovery from self-righteousness in the confidence that "Jesus is a great Savior"?

3. Read the section about Simon the Pharisee. (Pp 120-123; Kindle loc 1581-1625)

   📖 *Read the account in **Luke 7:36-50**.*

      Q What are the two shocking things mentioned in this story? Why would they have been particularly shocking to Simon?

      Q What about the sinful woman do you think would cause Jesus to say, in effect, "You should be like her"?

      Q As growing believers in Jesus, why do we have a <u>continuous</u> need to be "recovering Pharisees"—not to be content to remain Pharisees or assert the claim that we are "ex-Pharisees"?

4. Read the story of Paul's public rebuke of Peter. (Pp 123-125; Kindle loc 1629-1643) *[Also see the account in **Galatians 2:11-21**.]*

      Q Why did Paul have to call Peter out in front of everyone? What was at stake?

5. Q How does creating identities in anything other than Christ divide the body of Christ?

      Q Share how you have seen this in your own experience.

6. Q How does completely finding our identity in Christ through the cross make way for reconciliation?

7. 📖 Read the story of Ugandan missionary Florence Allshorn:

It's the story of Florence Allshorn, who arrived on the mission field in Uganda in 1920—a young unmarried English woman full of zeal to serve the Lord. She expected culture shock; she expected the climate to be a hard adjustment, she was prepared for primitive living conditions, but she wasn't ready for her fellow missionary. This woman barely welcomed her. Instead she made sure Florence understood that the house they shared would be divided down the middle and she was never to trespass over to her side or touch her things.

Florence was disappointed, but she got busy with her missionary work of teaching the young Ugandan women about Jesus and tried to ignore the situation. But she couldn't. She was plagued by bitter feelings toward this other missionary. Finally she sadly told her students she was leaving. One of them came to her afterwards in tears and said, "Everyone leaves us. You teach us that Jesus saves but we haven't seen him save this situation."

The situation that needed saving was the one that goes all the way back to the genesis of the family, to the deep divide between brothers, to the hostility of Cain. Nobody had ever been able to save that situation and as far as this young Ugandan woman could see, Jesus hadn't been able to save it either. Florence realized the reputation of the Lord was at stake, so she decided to stay and for an entire year read 1 Corinthians 13 every day, praying for a change of heart.

Eventually she was able to forget her own hurt and have some compassion for the other woman's loneliness. She wasn't sure how to break through the barrier so she just started doing little loving things like taking notice of what the other woman liked. She gave her a book she thought she might enjoy and chose special items from the market for her to eat. Eventually the woman's heart began to melt, and before it was over they had become true friends. Jesus had saved the situation.

Later Florence reflected,

Our modern world wants peace ... the church can go on exhibiting to the world (that this is the) place where that very thing it looks for is happening, little cases here and there of profound and real peace, in the midst of universal strife, and confusion…. Is it of blazing importance to us that they see this? Do we know in truth and in deed what really are the reconciling things? (Pp 128-129; Kindle loc 1704-1719)

Q How was Florence able to break through the dividing wall of hostility between her and her fellow missionary?

Q What actions or attitudes might you begin to employ to break through the dividing wall of hostility between you and someone else?

Q How does reconciliation bring glory to Christ? Why is that important?

TIME ALONE WITH JESUS: The heartbeat of the gospel is reconciliation through the cross. Ask the Lord to show you ways in which self-righteousness and/or creating identities other than in Christ are affecting your reconciliation with God or with others. Confess these ways to God, and ask him to tune your heart to the gospel so you can sing his reconciling song.

CHAPTER NINE

The Eyes of Jesus

1. Read the section about the Samaritan woman and Jesus. (Pp 131-134; Kindle loc 1726-1795)
   📖 *Read the account in John 4:1-42.*
   Q Where do you see the image of a bride and bridegroom in this story?

   Q Look up *Isaiah 61:10; 62:4-5; John 3:29; Revelation 19:7-8* and *21:2*. Record what you learn about how the Lord adores and adorns his bride.

2. Look through Jesus' eyes when he sees the Samaritan people from Sychar coming toward him at the well because of the woman's testimony. He says to his disciples, "Open your eyes and look at the fields: They are ripe for harvest." (v. 35)

   Q Where can you see, through Jesus' eyes, the harvest that is ripe in your own home or local community?

3. Jesus doesn't just show us the harvest; he invites us to be part of it.
   📖 Read *John 4:34-38.*
   Q What is Jesus' passion—his "food"?

Q In what way(s) do we enter into the labor of others engaged in the harvest?

📖 *"He knows this is the will of his Father and it is his meat and drink to do it—and he clearly wants us to be engaged in it with him. He wants us to have his eyes, to see what he sees, to be filled with his passion."* (P 134; Kindle loc 1792)

    Q Do you have Jesus' passion for the harvest of those who would come to Jesus for living water? Is there a particular "field" for which you have this passion? If so, which one?

4. 📖 *"It's the idols that steal our hearts away from Jesus and stall our passion. It's the idols that hold us back so we can't enter into the joy of Jesus' vision of the harvest."* (P 135; Kindle loc 1795)

    Q What desires (i.e.—honor, money, approval, etc.) might keep us from entering into the joy and passion of God's harvest?

5. 📖 *"But money isn't just tied to our desires; it's tied to our fears. Idols work on us from both directions."* (P 137; Kindle loc 1826)

    Q What fears (i.e.—security, safety, health, etc.) might keep us from entering into the joy and passion of God's harvest?

6. Janet realized that she had a struggle with the idol of her God-given artistic ability. (Pp 138-140; Kindle loc 1830-2397)

    Q How did Janet find repentance and liberation in the book of Hosea?

    Q How was her passion for art *"channeled into passion for Jesus and his kingdom and his glory"*?

7. Love is at the heart of idolatry.

    Q What was meaningful to you in the story about Marci and her idol of wanting children? (Pp 140-141; Kindle loc 1863-1882)

TIME ALONE WITH JESUS: *"Every good thing in life has this dual potential. We can either hold it tight or we can give it to him; we can worship it or we can worship him through it."* (P 140; Kindle loc 2397)

Of what "idol worship" do you need to repent?

Give your passion to Jesus for his kingdom and glory and ask him to help you channel your worship through it. Also, ask him to increase your vision and passion for his harvest.

CHAPTER TEN
The Dawn of an Expected Day

1. Read the story of the time immediately following Jeff's funeral. (Pp 145-146; Kindle loc 1925-1944)

   Q Why do you think the story of the demon-possessed son became so poignant for Charles and Janet at that time?

   Q What offered them the most hope and comfort in the midst of their grief?

2. 📖 Read *Isaiah 25:6-8*. Write all the promises in the space below.

   Q Which promise is most precious to you at this time?

3. The story of "Les Miserables" is one of the greatest redemptive stories of modern times.

   Q Consider how the character of Jean Valjean *"embodies this life of hope we're meant to live."* (Pp 149-150; Kindle loc 1989-2009)

4. *"The Lord uses our present sorrows to intensify our anticipation of that future joy."* (P 153; Kindle loc 2050)

    Q Share a time when you have seen suffering, grief, or disappointment—in yourself or another person— give a greater vision and intensify the yearning for the day of the Lord.

5. Q Share one or more thing(s) that the Lord has given or shown you in your life on earth as a foretaste of the future joy that awaits you.

TIME ALONE WITH JESUS: Look up and meditate on the following Bible verses and passages to intensify your anticipation of heaven and the Lord's return— *John 14:1-4; 1 Corinthians 15:23-24; Philippians 3:20; Colossians 3:4; 1 Thessalonians 4:15-18; Titus 2:12; 1 Peter 5:4; 1 John 3:2; Revelation 1:7; 3:11; 22:12, 20-21.* Record what you find in the space below.

CHAPTER ELEVEN
How Not to Miss Jesus

1. The chapter begins with the familiar story of two disciples on the road to Emmaus.
   - 📖 Read **Luke 24:13-35**. From this and the section on pages 157-159 (Kindle loc 2105-2137):
     - Q Where do you see the four ways we keep from missing Jesus in this story?
       a. Prayer (talking to a real person)
       b. The Word (opening the Scriptures)
       c. The Lord's Supper (breaking the bread)
       d. The fellowship (sharing Jesus with each other)

2. **PRAYER:**
   - 📖 *"Prayer is nothing more complicated—and nothing less wonderful—than a real person who's really with us."* (P 159, Kindle loc 2140)
     - Q What fresh images or new thoughts in the section on prayer (Pp 159-167; Kindle loc 2140-2255) remind you that Jesus is a person who's really with us?

   In order to have authentic prayer, not only do we have to realize that we are walking and talking with a real person, we must also <u>be</u> a real person, not *"thinking we have to get into a spiritual frame of mind and try to say the things Jesus wants us to say."* (Pp 162-163; Kindle loc 2189)
     - Q Why is it essential that you meet the real Jesus with the real you?

     - Q How does this change the way you pray?

3. **THE WORD:**
   - 📖 *"Jesus personally opened up the Scriptures to them and he will personally open them up to us."* (P 167; Kindle loc 2260) He "realizes"—makes the Word real—through his Spirit.

Q Share a time when he opened the Scriptures to you in a personal way.

📖 Dietrich Bonhoeffer wrote a letter to his brother-in-law, trying to explain how God actually speaks to us through his Word:

First of all I will confess quite simply—I believe that the Bible alone is the answer to all our questions and that we need only to ask repeatedly and a little humbly in order to receive this answer. One cannot simply read the Bible like other books. One must be prepared really to enquire of it. Only thus will it reveal itself. Only if we expect from it the ultimate answer shall we receive it. That is because in the Bible God speaks to us.... Only if we will venture to enter into the words of the Bible, as though in them this God were speaking to us who loves us and does not will to leave us alone with our questions, only so shall we learn to rejoice in the Bible....

And I would like to tell you now quite personally: since I have learnt to read the Bible in this way—and this has not been for so very long—it becomes every day more wonderful to me. I read it in the morning and evening, often during the day as well, and every day I consider a text which I have chosen for the whole week, and try to sink deeply into it, so as really to hear what it is saying. I know that without this I could not live properly any longer.

If it is I who determine where God is to be found then I shall always find a God who corresponds to me in some way, who is obliging, who is connected with my own nature. But if God determines where he is to be found, then it will be in a place in which it is not immediately pleasing to me.... This place is the cross of Christ and whoever would find him must go to the foot of the Cross ... this is the message of the Bible, not only in the New but also in the Old Testament. (Pp 168-169; Kindle loc 2269-2282)

Q What additional insight(s) do you get from Bonhoeffer's letter?

4. **THE LORD'S SUPPER:**
   Rose Marie Miller shares in her book a time when the "crack of the bread" during communion revealed Jesus to her. (Pp 170-171; Kindle loc 2315-2324)

Q What does the Lord's Supper communicate to you about Jesus?

Q If you can, share a time when Jesus revealed his love to you in a very real way while partaking in that meal. What was your response?

5. THE FELLOWSHIP:

📖 *"We're united and reinforced by each other's faith—because Jesus didn't just come to me; he came to you, too."* (P 171; Kindle loc 2330)

Q Recall a particular time when you felt Jesus' Spirit poured out when you gathered together in his name with other believers. How did it mutually encourage you or embolden you to share with others?

TIME ALONE WITH JESUS: *"Jesus said, 'I will come in and dine with you and you with me.' It's a two-way communion, a give and a take. We not only ask, we receive and give thanks. We offer him our lives from the depths of our hearts in gratitude for his love and for what it compelled him to do. We bow at his feet and tell him how glorious he is and how much we love him. We ask him to show us what he wants us to do. We give him ourselves."* (P 166; Kindle loc 2247)

What does the real you want to tell the real Jesus today?

What do you want him to show you?

What do you want to give him?

Beloved, don't miss Jesus. He's the ONLY one worthy of your life!